CUTIE CAKES & CUPCAKES

Simple, Relaxing, and Fun Coloring Books for Kids, Teens and Adults

Smart Lulu

INDIA · SINGAPORE · MALAYSIA

Thank you so much for buying my book! I appreciate your support. Before starting your coloring journey, please read.

For a great coloring experience, you can use different pressures with colored pencils or layer markers to create depth.

Paper quality is ideal for coloring with colored pencils and alcohol-based markers. **To prevent bleed-through and protect the next page, place a blank sheet of thicker paper behind the page you are coloring.**

Testing page:
Please check your color pens or markers on this page, to ensure a seamless coloring experience

Plated

Sliced

Stacked

Cherry on the cake

Lets Celebrate

Lets Eat

Party Time!

Sugar, Spice and Everything nice

Candles

Tiered

Queen of Hearts

Slice of Heaven

Two Hearts

Lets Jam

Checkered

For every milestone

Muffins Stand

Cherry Pie

Sweetest Occasion
ever!

Cakes & Roses

Lets Paint

Addictive

Cake & Wine

Perfect

Wedding Season

Topped with a smile

Sprinkles & more!

Ice-creams & cake

Mini cakes

Tea time!

Candies and cakes

Unique Occasions

Layers of Joy

Pie-Fect

Slice, Slice, Baby

Lollypop & candies

Kawaii!

All hearts

Donut Delight

Surprise me?